YOUR KNOWLEDGE HAS VALUE

Michael Frei

European Monetary Policy. Focusing on the Aim of Price Stability

GRIN Publishing

Bibliographic information published by the German National Library:

The German National Library lists this publication in the National Bibliography; detailed bibliographic data are available on the Internet at http://dnb.dnb.de .

Imprint:

Copyright © 2009 GRIN Verlag, Open Publishing GmbH
Print and binding: Books on Demand GmbH, Norderstedt Germany
ISBN: 978-3-656-93831-6

This book at GRIN:

http://www.grin.com/en/e-book/230776/european-monetary-policy-focusing-on-the-aim-of-price-stability

GRIN - Your knowledge has value

Since its foundation in 1998, GRIN has specialized in publishing academic texts by students, college teachers and other academics as e-book and printed book. The website www.grin.com is an ideal platform for presenting term papers, final papers, scientific essays, dissertations and specialist books.

Visit us on the internet:

http://www.grin.com/

http://www.facebook.com/grincom

http://www.twitter.com/grin_com

EUROPEAN MONETARY POLICY
FOCUSING ON THE AIM OF PRICE STABILITY

European Law and Law of international institutions

Author: Michael Frei

Index

Introduction

One of the most important objectives of the European Central Bank is the decision on its single Monetary Policy. The European Central Bank is the sole issuer of banknotes and bank reserves therefore the monopoly provider of the monetary base of an economy. This makes this institution the only one which has the needed instruments to make monetary policy. The ECB determined "price stability" as main intention of its policy because there is a contemporary consensus that inflation slashes the performance of economies strongly. The aim of this paper is to analyze why and how successful the European Central Bank has several instruments to achieve this important goal. The aim of this paper is to discuss the main goal of the European Monetary Policy and to analyze the instruments which can be used to maintain this goal. Finishing with a short evaluation about how successful the European Monetary Policy is.

European Monetary Policy in General

With the Introduction of a single Monetary Policy the member states of the European Union gave up a big part of their sovereignty. But with the introduction of the Euro as European currency, it was inevitable to introduce also a single monetary policy. This was a big and important step towards a unified Europe.

The European Central bank controls by its policy the cost of money, the supply of money and the availability of money. But the biggest problem of European monetary policy is that according to Monetary Theory, monetary and fiscal policy should always go together, in fact in Europe every state has its own fiscal policy and this policy is differing dramatically from state to state. To reach the general goals of monetary policy like employment and non-inflationary economic growth taxation has a very high importance. Regional inflation rates and growth dynamics still create divergence between the member states. This is the main critic point on the European monetary policy.

Importance of price stability

In article 105 (1) of the treaty establishing the European community "price stability" is determinate as main intention of the single European Monetary Policy (Eur-Lex). The aims of monetary policy are organized hierarchically; this means that price stability has overriding importance on all other objectives followed by the European central bank. After price stability is reached, the European Central Bank defines it at important to hold the employment rate high and to maintain economic growth constant. But this goal can only be achieved in a stable price environment. Generally leading economists assign such a high importance to a low inflation rate because of different motives. The Treaty establishes the maintenance of price stability clearly as the primary objective of the European Central Bank but it does not define exactly what is meant by price stability.

Therefore the European Central Bank had to find its own definition about what is defined as Price stability. Most economists of the ECB in 1999 concluded that a yearly increase in the Harmonized Index of Consumer Prices (HICP) on close to, but not over 2% can be defined as stable price environment. An increase over 2% would lead to a inflationary environment and an increase which is too high under 2% would cause in a deflation risk.

Since the "Great Inflation" of the 1970's it is widely agreed that inflation has to be under control to maintain economic growth and to have low unemployment. Before this time period the paradigm of tradeoff between high inflation rates and economic activity developed by A.W. Philips (1957) in which most Economists trusted in the 1960's gave Institutions the choice between different combinations of Monetary Policies. Philip's believed that high inflation would lead people to invest money, because in this case it's not productive to save capital anymore, this would result in an increase in output and higher wages. Thus considering this theory the negative effects of high inflation would be outweighed by the higher incentive to invest.

However this theory was well researched and proven by historical evidence, the Great Inflation proved that the relationship between high inflation rate and growth does not lead to the same result as stable prices do. In fact in the long run this relationship is negative. There are several evidences that the macro economical performance of a national economy diminishes when inflation increases (ECB Bulletin, 2008).

Furthermore stable prices for the consumers are very important to recognize relative price changes between goods and therefore to allocate monetary resources efficiently, without being perplexed by the changes in general price level through inflation. For consumer protection it is very important that the changes in real prices are easily comprehensible for everybody. Indeed the protection of consumers is very important for the trust of the Europeans in the European Union and its economic system.

Moreover price stability reduces the inflation risk premia in interest rates, as a consequence the real interest rate diminishes and a low real interest rate encourages people to invest because the return on investment has to always to be higher than the interest rate in order to make the investment attractive. One of the aims of the European Central Bank is to encourage companies and persons to invest, because investments maintain the real growth of an economy constant. The reason for this is that a cutback in investments like happening in a financial crisis runs the EU-Member countries into risk of stagnation or even recession.

Furthermore low inflation avoids unproductive activities made to safeguard against the negative impact of high inflation or a possible High inflation or deflation also leads to arbitrary redistribution of income and holdings and this weakens social security systems. In times of high inflation the wealth is distributed by the borrowers of money to the lenders, in times of inflation the same thing happens vice versa. The European Central Bank tries to avoid this arbitrary redistribution of wealth. To sum up a high number of investments, which are made typically in a stable price environment, strengthens the economy of a country and therefore in the case of the European Union, the whole Community (ECB, 2008).

To sum up, the benefits of price stability are economically very important. Therefore the European Central Bank has to use its available instruments to maintain prices stable.

Instruments to make Monetary Policy

Article 105 of the Treaty establishing the European Community states that in pursuing its objectives, the *Eurosystem "(...) shall act in accordance with the principle of an open market economy with free competition, favoring an efficient allocation of resources (...)"* (ECB, 2008). This is a very important point of the Treaty, because with the definition of the European economy as an open market economy with free competition the power of the state and therefore also of his institutions are very limited. In fact the European Central Bank has the assignment to don`t intervene too much in the local economies.

The European Central Bank has three main instruments to make monetary policy. The first and most important one are open market operations. The European Central Bank buys or sells assets, like gold, bonds and government securities to implement monetary policy. (Johnson, 2008). If the European Central Bank sells assets to other banks than the monetary base of the economy diminishes, therefore money is taken out of the market. On the other hand if the European Central Bank buys assets than the monetary base of the economy increases, this is called an expansionary monetary policy. With an expansionary monetary policy the inflation rate increases because the supply of money increases. While a non-expansionary monetary policy results in a decrease in inflation. Most of the supplied money is created or destroyed only electronically, the banknotes have only to be printed if demanded by the Member countries; this demand is very low in the time of credit cards and bank transfer, therefore the monetary base of the European economy is much bigger than the supply of banknotes.

The second instrument for the European Central Bank to make monetary policy is standing facilities. Standing facilities are used to absorb overnight liquidity and they bind overnight market interest rates. Moreover standing facilities signal the general stance of European monetary policy. The European Central Bank distinguishes between two different types of standing facilities, firstly the marginal lending facility, which allows national banks to provide liquidity to each other. The second one is the deposit facility, which allows counterparties to make overnight deposits with the National Central Banks (ECB, 2008). The European Central Bank sets the interest rate for transactions regarding this two standing facilities. With this overnight interest rate the ECB is able to control the so called price of money. A high price of money favors a low inflation rate and if money gets cheaper the inflation rate increases.

Furthermore the European Central Bank can set the minimum reserve requirements for banks, with this requirements the ECB can decide how much of its assets a bank is able to invest in the market. If Banks are allowed to invest high parts of their assets, the money supply for the market increases. On the other hand low minimum reserves assure the liquidity of a bank, in a financial crisis most banks run into liquidity problems. Therefore an expansionary monetary policy by the European Central Banks means higher susceptibility to crises. Through this instrument the ECB is able to control the liquidity of the money market.

To conclude, the European Central Bank has to be very careful in its chose of the right use to make Monetary Policy. It has to find the right mix between the three main Instruments to maintain the real inflation rate stable and to maintain growth stable. Because an increase in interest rates, made to fight too high inflation, diminishes economic growth and a decrease in interest rates, made to fight deflation, increases growth but holds the risk of a consequent hyperinflation.

Comparison with the Federal Reserve Bank in the U.S

According to Eurostat (2008) the European Central Bank reached its aim of stable prices only once in the last nine years. In the first three years after the single European Monetary Policy was Established, the inflation rate was between 2,4% and 2,5%. In 2002, the only year in which the ECB achieved its goal the inflation rate was about 1,8%. From 2003 to 2007 the real inflation rate was pending between 2% and 2,2% but with the financial crisis in 2008 it went up to 3,2%, this was the biggest fail of European Monetary Policy. For 2009 Eurostat estimated a real inflation rate of about 2,2%.

It is a very hard challenge for the European Central Bank to pursue its aim of stable prices because many different factors play along in the monetary market. The ECB follows a long-term strategy, in relation to the Federal Reserve Bank in the

United States, the European Central Bank sets its key interest rates higher, and this is connected to the aim of a stable inflation rate. In general the European Central bank makes fewer and lower changes in its key interest rate than the Federal Reserve Bank. The results of the European policy is a more stable interest rate, compared to the very fluctuating real inflation rates in the United States over the years and referring to the European banks which were able to coop better with the financial crisis than U.S. banks the European Monetary policy proved to be working more stable and therefore better than the American one (Le Heron, 2005).

Conclusion

The European monetary policy showed in the turbulent times of financial and banking crises, that it provides a high degree of stability to its member countries. The European Central Bank is an institution with a high reputation and also provides a forum for the national bankers and finance ministers to develop common strategies to fight recession and inflation. In the last years the inflation rates in the European Union, except in 2008, were very close to the main goal of stable prices.

Mainly countries which before the introduction of the Euro had volatile currencies are now in a more stable economic position. The common monetary policy also results fair competition between the member countries of the European Union because every country has the same monetary framework.

Sources

ECB, www.ecb.com Accessed: 05.01.2009.

ECB Monthly Bulletin, "Price *stability and growth*", May 2008.

Eur-Lex, http://eur-lex.europa.eu/en/treaties/dat/11992E/tif/JOC_1992_224__1_EN_0001.pdf, Accessed: 05.01.2009.

Eurostat, www.eurostat.com, Accessed: 05.01.2009.

Le Heron, Edwin. *"The New Governance in Monetary Policy: A Critical Appraisal of the Fed and the ECB"*, Bordeaux University Press, Berlin, 2005.

Johnson, Paul. Open market operations, Aurburn University Press, Aurburn, 2006.

Phillips, A. W. , *"The Relation Between Unemployment and the Rate of Change of Money Wage Rates in the United Kingdom, 1861-1957"*, Economica, 25. November, 283-299, 1957